*Night Boat & other poems*

Maria Barnas (1973) is a poet, writer, critic, and visual artist. She studied at the Gerrit Rietveld Academie and the Rijksakademie in Amsterdam. She won the C. Buddingh' Prize for her first collection of poetry, *Twee zonnen* (Two Suns, 2003) and in 2009 she received the J.C. Bloem Prize for *Er staat een stad op* (A City Rises, 2007). In 2014 her collection *Ja, ja, de oerknal* (Oh yes, the Big Bang), was nominated for the VSB Poetry Prize. She published a novel in 2017 *Altijd Augustus* (Always August) and in 2018 her poetry collection *Nachtboot* (Night Boat) appeared, for which she was shortlisted for the Netherlands' most prestigious poetry award, De Grote Poëzieprijs. In 2022 she published *Diamant zonder r* (Diamond without r), a sequence of poems about her Polish grandmother and the question of what mother tongue means, if a mother does not speak *her* mother's language. Her work has been described as 'contemplative, musical poetry, desperate and humorous, powerful and brittle, with a transparency that gets more complex on re-reading'.

Donald Gardner, born in London, is a poet and literary translator who divides his time between Amsterdam and County Kildare. Originally a Spanish-language translator (Octavio Paz, *The Sun Stone*, Cosmos Books 1969), Gardner has translated many Dutch and Flemish poets over the years. He published two collections of Remco Campert's poetry, *I Dreamed in the Cities at Night* (Arc Publications, 2008) and *In those Days* (Shoestring Press, 2015). For the latter collection he received the Netherlands' leading award for literary translation, the Vondel Prize. Gardner has published eight collections of his own poetry. His *New and Selected Poems (1966–2020)* appeared with Grey Suit Editions, London, in 2021.

Shearsman Books

# Maria Barnas
*Night Boat & other poems*

*translated from Dutch by*
Donald Gardner

First published in the United Kingdom in 2025 by
Shearsman Books Ltd
PO Box 4239
Swindon
SN3 9FN

Shearsman Books Ltd Registered Office
30–31 St. James Place, Mangotsfield, Bristol BS16 9JB
*(this address not for correspondence)*

EU AUTHORISED REPRESENTATIVE:
Lightning Source France, 1 Av. Johannes Gutenberg, 78310 Maurepas, France
Email: compliance@lightningsource.fr

www.shearsman.com

ISBN 978-1-84861-931-9

Copyright © Maria Barnas & Uitgeverij Van Oorschot
Introduction copyright © Rozalie Hirs
Translations copyright © Donald Gardner
Cover image *Night Swim* by Bobbye Fermie
Book design by Felix Salut

The right of Maria Barnas to be identified as the author of this work, and of Donald Gardner to be identified as the translator thereof has been asserted by them in accordance with the Copyrights, Designs and Patents Act of 1988. All rights reserved.

The publisher thanks Uitgeverij Van Oorschot, Amsterdam, for permission to publish this translation, and gratefully acknowledges the support of the Dutch Foundation for Literature.

Nederlands letterenfonds
dutch foundation for literature

# Contents

Introduction by Rozalie Hirs  8
Translator's Preface  11

From: *Twee zonnen* (Two Suns), 2003

Two Suns  15
Men  16
Sea of Beads  17
*Pianissimo très doux et très expressif*  18
A Table of Possibilities  19
*Erbarme Dich*  20
The Amstel  21
Night Wish  22
Paradise  23
Such Clarity  24

From: *Er staat een stad op* (A City Rises), 2008

Maudlin Metaphors are Hanging from the Bough like Dead Swans  27
It is Raining on the Frederiksplein  28
In Memory of Chengian Chen  29
A City Rises  30
Just to Make Sure  31
Continuity  23
The Space You Occupy  33
The Hands of the Clock in Hiroshima  34
Too Late  35
Mass  36

From: *Ja ja de oerknal* (Oh yes, the Big Bang), 2013

Thinking and the Girl   39
Extra Time   40
Children   41
~~Terribly~~   42
Vision   43
Goodbye, Amsterdam   44
Oh yes, the Big Bang   45

From: *Nachtboot* (Night Boat), 2018

Fresh Attempt   49
Looking for You   50
Future   51
*Gute Nacht Einsamkeit*   52
Night Boat   57
The Swimmer   61
Ideals   62
Middle   63
Moments   64
Shards of Me   65

From: *Diamant zonder r* (Diamond without r), 2022

It is important to be able to disguise yourself   69
Cz cz sz sz shh the mothers are only Polish   70
Only the dogs run here. They pant   71
I can tell a number of stories   72
I'm not saying I am Polish   73
I can speed along the motorway in pouring rain   74
In an online course I learned how to say sorry   80
Find a tune for the still warm heart   81
The wolves are growling under the table   86
You break up   87

Recent and uncollected poems:

Breaking Up Breaking   91
Ha-Ha   93
Night Ink   95
Song of the Garbage Man   98
The Borders of Europe   99

Acknowledgements   105

# Rozalie Hirs
## *Introduction*

M a r i a   B a r n a s is a poet who has also written prose and she is a successful artist as well. Not surprisingly her language is imbued with the mystery of how we perceive material reality. Art offers us a range of ways of looking at life. This can generate a sense of ambivalence and bewilderment in the mind of the reader and seemingly that of the poet too; the result however can be an expansion of one's horizons. Barnas attempts to find language for what she sees. Maybe this is why she is always in search of the narrative behind the poem or the poem beneath what she observes. This sets her work in the most important trend in contemporary Dutch poetry and poetry criticism, which is mainly concerned with the subject-matter and where the anecdote has pride of place.

Her first collection, *Two Suns* (2003) has as its motto *Die Nebensonnen*, Wilhelm Müller's poem, set to music by Franz Schubert as one of the songs in his *Winterreise*. *Nebensonnen*—sun dogs or parhelia—are an optic phenomenon, caused as we now know by the fragmentation of sunlight by ice crystals high in the upper atmosphere. At the time Wilhelm Müller knew nothing of this and this sight that he couldn't account for gave him a feeling of the *unheimlich*, the uncanny: he was glad when night fell and he could breathe again. By using his words as her motto, Barnas sets her collection in the context of inexplicable or disturbing observations; she locates them in a freezing winter, while referring to the sombre melody that Schubert composed for the poem. Even though her title poem, Two Suns, has summer as its background and most of the poems in this book have a light tone, we never quite lose that initial feeling. The main theme of *Two Suns* is relations with men and their shortcomings. The piano figures in a number of the poems, as it also does in her later collections: it is the instrument that is played on or it is abandoned by its player; or it is tuned by a piano tuner with beautiful eyes. It is slammed shut or else it won't go through a door when one is moving home. Finally, it is chopped in pieces during a ritual sacrifice.

In *A City Rises* (2007) Barnas continues her enquiry into the state of the world and the place in it of the I or the she. One has to find it and then occupy it—something that is not always straightforward. The best poems are like points of light amid realities that are ominous, to put it mildly. In terms of scope, tone and its refined style, *Oh yes, the Big Bang* (2013) can be compared with *Two Suns*. In it she speaks of the power of words, the power to be able to 'write the whole world'. She can taste the 'Big Bang' on her tongue. The notion that so enormous a phenomenon can be said in a word! These poems are relatively classical in form and style. The poet has children now and, even with all her practical worries, there is a playful, loving tone in these poems. We are witnesses to a psychological process. After her light-hearted journey through the cosmos, her next collection, *Night Boat* (2018) is 'a ship carrying the deepest black'; now she is sailing along the coast of fear and depression, night and the dark side of human existence. She returns to the England of her childhood years. The new reality of her life in Berlin is described in detail; the dominant mood is one of emptiness and solitude. There is something yet to be discovered; what it is, the poems don't tell.

*Diamond without r* (2022), Barnas's most recent collection, is an affectionate ode to her mother, her mother's mother and other family members from Poland. Barnas gives a voice to the silent victims of a war and to war trauma as it plays out in one family. Madness is close to home, becomes personal and acquires a name and voice. This key collection is a quest for identity and for the self. To quote Jacques Lacan and Luce Irigaray, both of whom are mentioned in Barnas's collection: a gulf has to be bridged, 'a chasm (...) between the self and the I'. The collection gives us idiomatic speech and written language across the generations. Languages as a social phenomenon. Words that give home to memories. We read, 'It is important to be able to disguise yourself / in another language. (...) It can save your life.' And, 'where was I when I was / in England between two languages / afraid of my own mouth.' Gradually it turns out that the grandmother is suffering from hallucinations and paranoid fantasies and is admitted to a psychiatric institution.

According to Lacan the scream, one's own or that of another, reminds one's own body, of previously uttered screams and the accompanying experience of suffering. One of the positive results is that we feel the pain again in our body, so that we can trace the message back to ourselves, and in this sense, 'understand' it. This process also reinforces the idea of the other as a separate entity. In the poem that opens with the line, 'Chop up a piano in blocks the size of dice', reality is confirmed by the scream, while the poet and the other are separated from each other. All the untidy realities, delusions and fantasies issue in a single massive scream in the form of a dance of the dead. This scream of the imagination reveals just how powerless the poet is: she has hacked her piano into little pieces and lugged it to Poland in a conspiratorial gesture, in order to resurrect the father of her grandmother, whom the latter has mourned so intensely, so he may play his trumpet once more. And with him, all the other dead and their musical instruments. A slightly earlier poem in the book shows how the reversal in the psychic reality of the poet had already begun as a sort of denouement. In this forceful gesture of Barnas's imagination, something occurs that is profoundly new.

The poems give us an insight into the therapeutic process of healing, through the unravelling of the hallucinations and stories that her grandmother told and contrasting these with the poet's own reality. In Barnas's work it operates retrospectively as if all the scraps of stories, nightmares and insights result in a coherent narrative so that she can continue on her way. And it is a way that moves one. Because the mind of the poet becomes palpably lighter, as a result of her uttering fragments of rediscovered languages—Polish and English—and her embracing the fears and delusions, her own and those of her grandmother, at the same time as she succeeds in identifying them. The poet shines the light on herself and her own narratives and sees them glow.

\* R o z a l i e   H i r s (Gouda, 1965) is a poet and composer. She has published nine Dutch-language books of poetry, including eight with the Amsterdam publisher, Querido. Her most recent collection, *ecologica* (2023) was awarded the prestigious Jan Campert Prize. Books of her poetry have appeared in various languages, including English, German, Spanish, Danish and Serbo-Croat.
\*\* Text translated by D o n a l d   G a r d n e r.

# Translator's Preface

Maria Barnas' witty and subversive poetry can be seen as a quest for an identity that always just eludes her: 'The floors / are buckling and the windows and doors / show cracks. These are the hinges / of an existence I call my own.' Nothing is what it seems for her and appearances are indeed just that—appearances. In another poem, she points out that, 'The corner of an eye can contain many things', and this could almost be taken as a mission statement.

Barnas is an artist and critic as well as a poet. In her poetry she asks how adequate language is to grasp what we see. Is one's native language a 'home'? How reliable is it and is it equal to the task of representing reality, above all the reality of our interaction with each other, that is undermined by ambiguity, personal history, as well as the secret passages of Freudianism. This enquiry comes to a peak in her most recent collection, *Diamond without r*, in which she investigates her Polish roots as well as her adolescent years spent in Oxfordshire. Polish words and scenes are held up to the prism of her lines, and there are also fragments of English, which may comprise flashbacks of her English experience.

For the reader this poetry has an unstable character; it expresses an urgency to belong as well as a sense of rejection, a desire sometimes to say two, contradictory things at once. It is at times quizzical, defiant and mocking.

As a translator, it may have been just this elusive, teasing character of her work, the instability as it were, that was the challenge, and made her work such a pleasure to turn into English. One doesn't want one's poetry to be easy.

I first worked for her when she was reading at Poetry International in Rotterdam 2008, and I have translated sets of her work ever since for various events or literary journals, until suddenly I realized I had enough poems for a collection. It has been a pleasure working with her. Her English is excellent and as a result, we have always batted my translations back and forth; indeed, it has sometimes felt like two for tennis, especially when she unexpectedly dropped a last-minute change just over the net. These are translations, not versions, and I hope I've succeeded in following this moving target. I believe the volatility of speech, written and spoken, to be the underlying theme of her work. I hope my English will convey the spirit, the mental courage and even what I think of as the gaiety of this deeply original Dutch-language poet.

Donald Gardner
10 June 2023

# Two Suns

(2003)

# Two Suns

When I fall asleep the sea is still below
and the sun as always ahead.

I am next to a detail of dark water
and I'll be by the boats later on

their white sails light as relieved voices,
ecstatic now and then between the chattering gulls.

But in the ring I was given I am set slanted
next to a date. And I see him disappear in the distance
with a sun. Sloppily repeated in the window.

He called me Flower. Also Springtime, Sexy, Sweetest,
Sweetie, Sweet and recently more often
Prefernot, Notnow, Please.

# Men

I think of the man I loved.
Do I love him?
How many fears does that make?

Our plates became emptier
and on the edge a flower, cut
from a radish. A small exuberant life.

Not meant to eat, he knows.

# Sea of Beads

The town turned round
when I looked back. Excuse me please
I thought you were someone else.

I've got a good swearword
a mean bead on my tongue.

I cut a striped heart out of paper.
Don't I dare that I need you?

The world is tired and on the blue lines
of an exercise book it's cold.

First a man still slept here.
Now the body rises.

## *Pianissimo très doux et très expressif*

Flames are raging round a tower.
A black angel with a suitcase jumps
from a window on the 37th floor. What is he
taking with him?

I play *Rêverie* on the piano. *pp très doux et très
expressif.* But how must I.
I turn off the sound on the telly.

The black angel jumps to his death once again
and I need a reason to live I believe in.
But you'd see it too if you closed my eyes:
it is dark inside my head.

There is a tower collapsing here
and everything is gentle and expressive
as an eyelash blown from a fingertip.

# A Table of Possibilities

I took the table to work on.
The legs came off easily and the top isn't heavy
but now I'm sitting at the window on the wrong side
of this house, the city escapes me. A face
I don't remember the name of.

Maybe I shouldn't listen to a requiem
in the morning but otherwise I hear girls
giggling. You never know when they'll start.
Can't the singer make a single mistake just for once? Like me

with a tall man in a low house on the water.
We swam. We were happy once in a while
but one day I became frightened of the table.

It made no difference if I left.
It would still be there.

He shows the new woman the little sun
on the thermostat to be switched off at night.

Does she know she's sleeping under my blankets?
That the bed is mine and that I'm on my way
to collect the chairs and the bad sea.

## *Erbarme Dich*

An Englishman with gorgeous eyes is tuning my piano.
I'm going to do it very carefully, he says.
Droplets and leaves are spilling from the elderberry bush
in the corner of the garden, sir, like words from my mouth.
Would you mind?
I think the tree is incurably ill.
We might have a slight problem here.
We.

A humid summer has dawned in my mind
dear sir, a paralysing heat. Do you know what to do?
I don't know what 'verzengend' is in English.
Would you like a drink?
Thank you so much.
How much?

In Brussels I ate chocolate wrapped in gold foil
and I wore an impeccable hat.
In Paris I rode in a Ferris wheel.
I could go with you to London just like that.

If I have sugar. And milk.
The Englishman plays.
*Erbarme dich.*

That's that. That's all.
Thank you so much.

# The Amstel

The water of the Amstel wears silver,
reflects space on the windows of the tram.
It is just the front of the city

but everything I say exists.
Has already taken shape before I find the words
and the pigeons spread their wings, noisily
shake their airy skirts.

My nights consist of nothing but days
that don't arrive and I can't sleep
for fear of missing out on life.

# Night Wish

How am I supposed to lie down
in the bed of a livid man?
That's how I've made him.

I never stopped asking him
to finally leave me alone.

Are you leaving?
Do you want me to leave?
What are you still doing here?
If you break up with me one more time,
I'll break up with you.

But before you go. What exactly did you mean
by Fuck you a thousand years.

# Paradise

To impress the actor at my table
I say that the best film I ever saw is called *Paradise Lost*.
The camera was static and everything was b & w
strange as a paradise, no, stranger.

The man says I mean *Stranger than Paradise*.
I focus on the letters of 'reserved'
until they start swimming and the world is a blur.

A clay head is shoved into an oven
and is heated with shame so hot the head turns
solid, small as a clenched fist.

But an image is brittle
and I don't believe that of the world.

I can't utter it.
It's more something for an actor.
He gets up. A world awaits him.

I'll stay for a bit.

# Such Clarity

He pours white clouds in my glass
of blue sky. Blocks of ice tinkle in the landscape
and the day is a table for two.

# A City Rises

(2008)

## Maudlin Metaphors are Hanging from the Bough like Dead Swans

There is a life that withdraws from the subject
at dinner slowly grows inwardly

and although my voice box reiterates a laryngeal
gets entangled in itself (that bird-black

and that your thoughts of a tree consist of this
a flock that cannot think of a better place)

won't listen because everything recalls
would you like white and points towards

or red but my fear that it isn't a flock at all
is greater than my dread of death

yes red please.
Game soup is served.

Can someone chase away these lonesome swans?
They cut figures of eight in the waterway.

Then I will let the night tree take root in me
and sway. Seek images for serene.

I spill birds on the tablecloth.

# It is Raining on the Frederiksplein

She is standing on the edge of what is just about
to happen and the surrounding trees grow

rigid. She folds up promises to others
and spits two words in the unyielding

white water. A dog jumps
over the edge as it begins

to rain in the fountain.
Love had to do with it

but it is only language that is inclined.
And inclines.

Fountains make similar gestures
and the dog will shake itself out of its coat

if things go on like this. Her hand wavers
and where her words reach the water

two dogs begin to dawn.
One without coat the other without heart.

# In Memory of Chengian Chen

Chengian Chen (1947–2006) lived illegally in The Netherlands. When
a fire broke out in the hostel where he lived, he jumped to his death out
of a second-storey window.

Houses with towers of prices and slanting
beams in the display window back gardens
sun doors opening out and a silver bus
driving into a future; neither the umbrella

with its heart burst open in the wastepaper basket
nor the jaded palm plant on the ground floor
can support me. Can't someone get rid of it,
faded and broken it adorns nothing and no one.

Like rain I will fall down the façade and set
a foot in the void. If they ask me who I am
I tell them the smoke drives skies in my heart.

They say that they didn't know me
but if they must they'll show you
where I lived: where no one answers.

# A City Rises

From the top storey into the city.
The streets of Buenos Aires are roaring below.

The city where everything turns out right.

They take you along in angles.
But shadows are blowing here

and pebbledash buildings
swirl. There is one

with a heart of grazed red stone.

And to avoid seeing a heart
you go downstairs. Keep your shadow close.

The red hem round your neck opens out
into a red river. Think waterfall.

Waterfalls.

A piano lid slams a house shut.
Swipes a building against the wall.

In the lift you stumble over the threshold from a certain house.
A ceiling of stars ascends.

Twenty storeys plunge. Full length.
A city rises.

# Just to Make Sure

July 8, 2005 LONDON — London struggled back Friday after bombings. Much of London was eerily quiet. Bombed stations were shrouded in security curtains, and refrigerated trucks waited outside to cart away bodies.

The streets are stirring all the same. Interrupt me.

Although we wormed our way out of the city along the Thames
in tremendous curves we were prepared for everything.

Feel free to leaf through the storeys, a dog-ear
in the shaft of a lift. Make thick leaden drops out of metal
and plunge in nosedives. Pitfalls.

Capital letters hardly keep up with the bombs.
Mistake me.

They are carried like sandwiches in Tesco carrier bags
where I—here we go.

We were ready we were prepared
and we stayed eerily quiet.

We had planned the pits well before
and meticulously scraped ruins of streets and houses
out of stone. Sliced a shell out of square
just to make sure and hacked stairs
out of underground steps in the opposite direction.

Someone doubted it but when the time came it began.

The bombs landed in their place.

# Continuity

The girl ascends the staircase.
The girl ascends the staircase with steps

that jostle into a curve at the top. She keeps on walking
despite the fact that she can't do anything about it.

We get a glimpse of her forehead, pale skin
her hair parallel to the steps.

She looks straight ahead while ascending the staircase.

There's a girl ascending the staircase!
It could be a wig the way that hair's hanging.

She holds a parcel tightly under her arm.

There's a parcel going up the staircase the steps
a door on the stairs on the steps the ankles the girl.

She doesn't change now her toes have reached the winding steps

a fan over her head a door swings out of the dark
out of the silence in her a curve is wrung steps shoulder-high.

A girl is ascending the staircase with a reason.

# The Space You Occupy

The rocks will have to turn carefully into deer
on the ridge of the hill. Ragged and blacker every night.

The sheep run as a white stain a hand wipes a piece of peel
from the table no from the grey

meadow. Startled by the huge irresolute
creatures. How the hill in the water—

My mother moves as a memory
moves as my mother in the uncertain garden.

Not true: she rinses out a room of glass.
I have her questions:

Do you wake up sometimes
startled by memories that drip on your forehead
till they become facts. They repeat

your name incontrovertibly a street a number and a country
to write on the back of an envelope.

That you are a woman and what that means no you
as you blow-dry the morning and puff a lock

of the past from our forehead with a sigh. You comb knots
from my hair. Don't move. We are so alike.

Where were we? There
they are on the right. No those are stones.

# The Hands of the Clock in Hiroshima

They stand on the tower to watch
a horse being dragged to the water.

Where do you bury death? They point at the creature
and will shake it from their fingertips.

They have been motionless for sixty years.

The photo the explosion made wiped everything
white except the shadows of those who kept staring.

We have gained a city.
Everything gleams and is dust-free.

We have stared at the hands on the tower.
They didn't blink.

We have shaken the bells.
We asked the man who synchronizes them who

did this. Who has done this?

The horse brings on ever more history.
They say it prances since it refuses to shrink.

# Too Late

I was cycling across a lull in the city
that turned slowly into houses where people live together
when loneliness jumped on the pillion

and said I'll ride with you a bit I'm going that way anyway.
It's not convenient I said. I have to find a beginning
for a letter. Goodbye.

I peeled a red apple and saw the pale
flesh looking so withdrawn on its plate
I couldn't eat it. Imagined the woman

you preferred and thought of another
country to live in.
Loneliness had tried out all the chairs

and was just lying down in bed when you called.
You looked so weary I could have invited you in.
But you had lots of stuff. Suitcases full

of nimble words too heavy to carry.
The man speaks. Why won't you let me in
is there someone else in there?

No, I lie. I'm on my own. I count how many
lies a person can come across in a doorway
and get the feeling something's missing.

# Mass

We are the oarsmen with dew on our faces
rowing into the morning without a sound.
We are the ones whom newspapers proclaim
whom statistics speak of, who are in the frame.
We are the risk that you spread.
We've found each other and we'll only be quiet
when we know what the hell we're here for.

Might you perhaps have anything to do with it? Are you the one
who undermines us; makes us pine away in randomness
because we are so many: our wailing
will never be so loud as the scream of a woman
whose hands burn on the tram rails.
There she is. She is screaming as a woman
screams whose hands are burning.

The louder we make ourselves heard the more we
destroy ourselves and later we're the incomplete ravens
of ink in the palm of your hand that you shake
as if it were a stranger's in the last light.
Where are they going the oarsmen move
unnaturally backwards they beat the oars
wide as the water and retreat along the land.

# Oh yes, the Big Bang

(2013)

# Thinking and the Girl

In the corner of my eye fields and houses go past
while I try to focus on the girl sitting opposite me.
The corner of an eye can contain many things.
A house that I recognize a ditch a cow and even

the way the creature grazes and stares
stretching its neck stressed out by a strange sound.
Or is it more rigidly awaiting a signal?
Animals proliferate at the edge.

Settle down in this subsiding marshland
with ungainly houses in every one of which
I've lived. The girl is clasping a book

in her lap with cross-sections of brains. She draws
circles round lobes and ventricles and dissects
my ability to think and think of her.

## Extra Time

And just when everything seems right
the children the plants the newspapers
the grass the washing-up almost
coats hanging shoes matching

and you want to draw a breath
in the corner of your eye a multitude lifts off
from their seats in a stadium. They rise
as one man. Lift their arms and cheer.

How ten-thousand tongues move
as in one toothless gob. Men slide round
the field and behave according to the rules

inside the lines and outside governed by a ball
and a penalty spot. The world is so close
you could wipe the sweat from Robben's brow

and you see fury rolling in Ribéry's eyes. Tenacity
in their calves till the cameras sway
and a crowd sinks back again into its seats.

And just as you're about to exhale
more surely than rules and lines a chill
rolls into the house among the bodies

that slowly and repeatedly rise gasping
for sound around our feet. We stay seated.
Pitting our hopes on extra time.

# The Children

Still thirteen minutes
no, twelve.

I had the whole day to work in
but I started reading and sorting things and seeing
how I could best plan my day and now
there's only eleven.

Then I have to pick up the children. Put on nappies
wipe noses and shout that they mustn't hit
heads with saucepans or kick
animals and doors or poo on the carpet
and then ride through the poo on the toy train
and don't wipe your nose on your brother
and now you really must sleep sleep please sleep now
in your own bed and not shriek not shriek don't shriek like that!

Sobbing in me
as I see the morning go by
in shock shocking.

Still eight minutes for a masterpiece
or at least a start.

Something that might sound like this.

## ~~Terribly~~

In Lochem you can come across Catholic fish
that swim around in circles in a bowl
on a window sill in a classroom
in St. Joseph's School. Miss Mol

hangs up a sign with plant for plant.
Table for table. Chair for chair.
Fish for fish. I couldn't believe my eyes.
I could write the whole world.

When I left to live in Amsterdam for ever
I wrote to Miss Mol that I'd miss her.
I'm still waiting for a letter. Perhaps

I shouldn't have crossed out the word 'terribly'.
The trees of the forest that began in the garden
gleam through the houses on the Cremerplein.

# Vision

Salt and pepper mills roll off the table. Ashtrays smash
in splinters on the ground and red wine spills
from shattered glasses on the lime-green lounge cushions
that cover the breaking sundeck planks.

While menus scatter like startled seagulls
over the Kostverloren canal, I narrow my eyes.
One person after another leaves the table as if prearranged
until I alone am left to witness a ship chug past.

On the ship a hill of wrecked bicycles.
As the skeletons reach the bridge I recognize
A certain ending in the wreckage. The deathbed drifts by.

I hold onto whatever it is the skipper must see
when he vanishes under the bridge. Could this be a vision?
You never know. Slowly it passes by.

# Goodbye, Amsterdam

When I look along the quay I see a night
entering the city like a long sloop
searching for cover in the grime of a shallow
river. The Amstel flares up and fades

in my memory while the water sloshes
against the banks. I don't have to stay.
I can bear all names. Cross all rivers.
What else do they convey but the deepest gravel

the most stifling past so densely packed
that flawless moments may emerge.
Happiness any old day. When it gets grey
and almost light there is a wavering name.

A city. Time without shores and I.

# Oh yes, the Big Bang

Oh yes, the Big Bang I catch myself saying.
How can this fit in my mouth?
The origin of life a lump on my tongue.

Hush. Fear is a flock that rests in a tree.
Or are words huddling in the branches
black as ink. It is a form of panic

that wells up in me and bursts from my throat,
a flock dispersing. The cosmos spreads
its wings. We flutter and screech.

# Night Boat

(2018)

# Fresh Attempt

I am not a painter, I am a poet.
Why? I think I would rather be
a painter, but I am not.
—Frank O'Hara

Through a chink in the door I sum up the room
at the level of a retreating horizon.

Loops and lines shoot alongside vanishing points
to depict an escape route.

Look, calculations can be measured: weigh them
in a hand that you clench and strike the table

with a fist. Listen to its sound
echoing in the room next door.

Close a door to make something happen—
a form of certainty in the discoloured

house that has shifted slightly. The floors
are twisted and the windows and doors

show cracks. These are the hinges
of an existence that I call my own.

# Looking for You

All I know is you had a cat flap
in the kitchen door. The cat preferred it outside.

I had one like that myself.
I was walking through the city at night and saw

you streets away from home. I called
but you acted as though you didn't know me.

Later I saw you looking for something in a bush.
The traffic was swirling in all directions.

I grabbed hold of you.
Won't you come to me.

You scratched my face open
and then I saw that you weren't mine.

We don't listen. Don't answer.
No name no kitty litter no collar

round the neck with waterproof
address tag to deter us.

Hear the fearful bells peal out.
We will find rest

in how a wary creature becomes us.
We won't be caught.

# Future

An office chair rolls off stumbling.

I could say to the dull mirror: you are this fish.
And what's more: you shall adore me oh dearly beloved
why are you gasping like that, yearning on the surface?

We could say: the future is a dull blackened mirror.
Or: there is a future that we design
with fat lazy fish

to immerse in heavy water and to scoop up
like dark rubies to hoard in the bank
or safe with the words under your mattress.

Besides, you can pet the rays in the oceanarium.
They turn their fins towards your finger tips

that rehearse shapes of a future
on a screen on which light barely breaks.

## *Gute Nacht Einsamkeit*

It's the day I've started writing
in books in pencil admittedly
but one with a sharp point
and definite in various ways.

*Der Untergeher* is the first novel
I read in German.
In the margins I place
possibilities as in a vase.

It's the language that I make my own
as I gather words in *Kreuzberg*.

It's in the *Nostitzstraße* that I find plenty.
*Gute Nacht Einsamkeit ich bin so gern allein mit dir*
someone has written in neat letters on the wall
by the cocktail bar where men don't enter
only women who look like girls.

It's the city I don't mind living in
but I get stuck at *Klavierradikalismus*.

    *

In the *Nostitzstraße* I also read: *Kohle und Holz*
in flaking Gothic letters.

Every day in a cellar with things swimming in things
I enquire about the price of the orange lamp
a globe in a globe that shifts like a planet's shadow
around the little man who says *heute dreißig Euro*.

I don't even have half of that
in my pocket to buy ham for my husband
raw slices of life
from the Black Forest.

*

I'm curious what *Tchibo* bargains I'll find
on the shelves in *Kaiser's* and can't choose
between the double-sided mug
the bra with transparent plastic straps
and the socks with knobs so you don't slip
and so that you feel safe generally
even if you don't have a slippery floor
because you'd rather your kids cycle
along the corridor and through the linking
rooms than down the *Gneisenaustraße*
that takes you to the end of Germany
roaring and without any detours.

*

I bounce a few words
at *Kita Sonnenschein* where pre-schoolers
are discouraged from doing difficult puzzles
and Yussuf with the ginger curls and dazzling
smile hugs my knees
and asks if he can go with me
while his mother is right beside him
and there's a smell of sour cauliflower soup.

The kindergarten teacher doesn't wash and why should she
she's already been smelly a long time and her hair sticks to her
skull so she doesn't have to comb it.

*

Write: that I'm happy
with a sharpened pencil and a book
from the *Berliner Büchertisch* that's as good as new
which I can slowly get lost in.

I can see that this is also avoiding life
from the grey women who are hidden in the *U-Bahn*
behind an open book.

When they stop reading a moment
for instance to scoop a chocolate-coated muesli bar
out of the carrier bag between their second-hand
shoes I detect to my alarm
a barely perceptible knowing wink.

*

I'd like to know which life I avoided
because between the lines
of Berlin I read nothing but emptiness.

On my way to the *Viktoriapark* past the watermelons
into a street that sneaks uphill past fairytale villas
and an ivy-clad wall says that Konrad Zuse
lived there I get the idea that change lies ahead.

I become mildly hopeful as I walk along the *Kita*
with the *Streichelzoo* where you have to register
your children before they're born
and take the back entrance into the undulating park

where everything that simmers and ferments and everything
radiant and magisterial in Berlin converges
in the ruler-straight waterfall bordered with boulders.

I can't see if the waterfall is real.
Somebody made it up.

The park that's supposed to be wild and romantic
as though Goethe might ramble here is wild and romantic
because no one does any weeding or scoops up shards.

The woman who smashes bottles on the paths
and against the cars round the edge of the park
screeches she's coming to get us.

\*


I'd rather not go to the *Bergmannstraße* today
because I'm afraid that a man will be there
at the doors of the *DM* who knows things about Jesus
with all that implies but I have to
get my photos of the waterfall printed.

There he is. Legs splayed.
Heaven glugging in his throat.

With the growing dread
that reality is burying me alive

I deny that the world has been made up
and that I skulk around in this story
like a slow reader.

And I've not even mentioned
the futuristic park between the railway tracks
with the slippery grass and the joggers
who run rectangles instead of laps.

\*

Or the house with the *S-Bahn* cutting
right through its ground floor.

Or the museum of technology where you can throw
all your loose change into a top-speed turbine
and nobody knows what for.

Or the *Prinzenbad* where you stand
in one bobbing mass body to body
that fills the pool corner to corner like plums
on a *Torte* with heads that laugh languidly
and timidly at such intimacy to eat *Pommes*
afterwards with tea from a real mug
and no one else covers their naked tummies.

\*

The pale thighs of the dreary women
lie like flat loaves on the plastic chairs.

When they rise slowly
the reading chairs stand there like cities
with someone else's life imprinted in the skin.

The women wrap me up loosely
in a quick-drying towel from *Tchibo*
and go off with me under their arms.

\*

Leave me alone
I'd like to say to someone

If there was anybody
to whom I could say Leave me alone.

# Night Boat

    I

I saw a ship carrying the deepest black
from which something flares up

like a face in a memory.
It is the darkness of the blinded

who swim so long in a cell
that they see colours or find them.

They explore the wall with webbed hands
in search of substance in light.

I make moments out of time
by closing and opening my eyes.

The cargo that trawls through the water
guards what is to come. Always

earlier than I thought and later the boat
carrying nothing but night glides by.

II

I move between a boat and its description.
Between these boats there is space.

I can fall into it. Or jump
as from the white cliffs of Dover and never

hit the ground. A reality is visible from my chair—
do I get closer if I shove my chair forward?

I want to see what happens when I tilt
the chair backwards—

a body appears.
It moves slowed down by a layer of snow.

It announces something and sooner turns away
Swirling is a word that welcomes the body.

Above all swirling.
And strikes it out.

### III

A faltering boat in me is meant to bring me
home from the open sea.

I don't ask what is the time
because whoever is wearing the watch

might hazard a guess about the nature of time
and continue about the unknowable

in general. There are countries
in the distance to go and live in.

Only the boat turns white.
What surrounds me remains black

and sloshes sea-like.
Snow is falling and spoken snow falls.

Snow is falling
in awkward flakes from my mouth.

## IV

I can say that I have no longing
to return to the island

to climb the tree that doesn't stop
raining. The smell of soil and leaf

lures me to the land that I don't miss
but that breaks me up. Breaking.

I run round the house to be before
time and ahead. Take a breath

rewinding *Back to the Future*
and—fast forward to see the DeLorean—

when I pause Michael J. Fox.
He looks as if he's also always too late

and regrets everything in advance.
I will take the night boat and be awake.

# The Swimmer

There is someone who wants to swim home.
He swims in a straight line

through swimming pools ditches a fountain
and doesn't speak to anyone about sea

or homesickness. He speaks to no one.
There is a hollow in him like a shallow cellar

in which he buries a horse alive.
He shakes up the soil.

If the creature lies on its side
and holds its breath, it fits exactly. Breathe in!

There is a hollow like a cosmos in which you can
fall and fall till it no longer matters

where you are from. There is the horse
that stretches its legs shakes off the stink

of people and billows out to sea.

# Ideals

I have always heard it proclaimed everywhere
that this is your abiding place: behind the mountains.
Go back home, Poetry, and take me with you.
—H.H. ter Balkt, *Ga naar huis Poëzie*, 2007


I turn over women who want to accept their body
as it is and I tear out suggestions

for a valley orgasm that can save relationships.
Do I want to save my relationships?

They no longer count calories and embrace curves.
Next to them a slender body

living on linseed that swims in ocean water.
Others wearing colonial colours hunt

a wild beast under the shade of palm trees
off the page. It starts to growl in me.

I read that Poetry dwells behind the mountains
which must also be somewhere.

This way a landscape takes shape
I see a figure entering it.

It starts strolling past brooks and bridges
like an eye taken in by a painted landscape.

I might well be that shape looking
for love in the form of a body.

This way I am driven.

# Middle

And if the day came
When I had a natural emotion
I'd get such a shock I'd probably lie
In the middle of the street and die
—Morrissey, *Nowhere Fast*, 1985


I listen to my body
but don't understand it.

Maybe it is too pale.
Does it pour too hard from the head

too cold full of squashed-flat
thought braids gushing

and does it splash from the arms
tautly so as not to touch the curtain

the tiles the joints weary
of the search for lives in other

bodies. While the soap roars
a prelude in the waste pipe

the body speaks so we move
strange estranged

and I see more and more bodies
estranging themselves from me.

# Moments

That someone on waking asks: Can you find the beginning?
That someone is your son.
His hand still warm from sleep.

That time expands in the shape of a star
towards all the instances when things easily came unstuck
or not. The line of moments tears apart.
The plastic groaning and made of whale
or was it rabbit-glue.

Let go!

That someone is a man who laughs
when you ask why are you laughing.
Rolls over.

The blanket speaks: I'm not laughing.

The reality is a roll of sellotape
you hear.

I can't find the beginning.

# Shards of Me

On the way to a different day
the meadows wind and sun-drenched

a woman blocked my path.
She said there is glass

on the path so fine
you almost don't see it

there where the trees begin
can you see it glittering?

And the trees began
they began everywhere

when the woman cycled on
with the smile of someone

who has done a good deed
and I was too late

to ask if she was protecting me
from the shards of a stranger

or if she enjoys smashing
bottles on the path

that was starting to show cracks.
Slow plants crept over my feet.

I saw wrinkles in my skin
and heard voices in me squawking.

Something with short wings
rose out of my throat.

In between the shards
it lit up.

# Diamond without r

(2022)

It is important to be able to disguise yourself
in another language. You tie up
a scarf full of poppies
that bleed into each other
around your head.

It can save your life.

I jump on a trampoline
as I see other children
jump who don't look
at how other children
fail to keep time

fall

do I want shall
I not tell you

that at night I'm buried
under bodies in a pit.
Someone whispers don't move
or they'll shoot
if I open my eyes I don't know
what

we disappear into
when we go and look
at screeching children and entire
families in the depths
of a steaming wave pool

Cz cz sz sz shh the mothers are only Polish
behind the closed kitchen door.

They chop up rumours sharpen the knives
make a broth from a two-headed
monster no one will miss

me

I

am so happy so happy my nose is in front
and when I ask with my sobbing nose
if it's true that I've smelled death
in a dream that infuses everything
they hang half an onion round my neck
as a medal and not to the side.

Where are their mothers?

They talk to black and white cowboys
knit socks in the colours of Douai
and Gladbeck that no one will wear
where coal in abundance
where nie placz no one

in the corridor cupboard with the weeping
door that recalls Katowice
when they think no one can hear them
in nights that turn grey

Only the dogs run here. They pant
to get to the edges faster
than cars that dissolve as soon as you're

close they almost hit me in passing
yes I know the tale of the horizon.

It comes from the shrubs where Kim sits
snorting glue or from behind the bus shelter
where the rapist hides in himself.

We don't know for sure if he exists.

Usually it's someone you know
the mothers say. What does he see
that makes him sway like a stag
with antlers that are too heavy?

The dogs run to string all the suburbs
together to make a single city. And they go on
running for the sake of the blood that keeps on pulsing
and recalls a heart that clots.
And because nobody else does it.

One day they'll bring the heart
like a jewel of pure cosmos
back home on the tongue.

Am I chasing the dogs? In the heart
that is missing I am
a suburb

I can tell a number of stories
about where I am from.
While I am telling them they are true
where was I when I was
in England between two languages
afraid of my own mouth.

Even people who live in the countryside
that is no lowland dream
of life in the countryside
I have seen them with my very eyes.

What am I to do with the hills that roll
and the man who hesitates on the verge
who went to mow a meadow?

Where do I come from? I don't know
why I only find the beginnings
of an answer in this place
that is not my mother's or her
mother's mothers

mom

I am at the verge of
I am at a verge
I am a verge
diverging

tongue

I'm not saying I am Polish
even if it's only from the ground to the knee
just like my mother to her navel
never says she is Polish just as my granny
denies she has a Polish-German accent.

I'm not saying I am English
just because I was a child on that island
that withdraws ever further

homesickness a hammock
I no longer fit in.

I don't say I am Dutch too tall
from hormones they inject the calves
that nobody touches anymore high
from their chemical shit through the throat
if they are not slaughtered straightaway
to make them grow fast and cheap

no one knows what hormones
look like do they have calyxes excess
growths or tendrils inducing breasts
also with males those milksops.

I don't say that it is only mleko rolling
on my tongue that betrays my throat

you can rock in it till the sickness
unmoors a ship that wait! doesn't
wait for me

I can speed along the motorway in pouring rain
with children in the back seat and sing so loud
so as not to think of a wrong
movement that would shut us up all at once

that my voice isn't in tune
unreliable like the windscreen
in which with a crack a star appears
with lightning bolts that clinch shards together

that I don't know the song
I make up words
that don't fit the rhythm.

stary niedźwiedź mocno śpi
stary niedźwiedź mocno śpi

I take a gulp and don't look back
To avoid the star that branches on the foreheads
of the sleeping children

that I am not the song

I can eat fish and say I'm a vegetarian
because I no longer eat any chickens or pigs
or sheep or cows.

I like to look the animals in the eye
but they don't respond when I get off my bike
utter a sound. There is only one sleeping boar
that recognizes something in me. I mustn't wake him

dance on my toes
because of something heavy
that had best stay out of sight

I can clasp a watermelon
on the back seat like a globe
and not go on about a head
and how it is split. The meat
bruised the half skull shaking
in my hands and holding it upright
in my lap while the car bumps along a dirt road
full of potholes so that nothing splashes
over the edge looking in the rearview mirror
to see if I make a good impression

Are you sure you don't want any meatballs
in your soup? Shall we start up a commune
for likeminded

Likeminded?

who are also against pollution
and for opening borders. Likeminded
lumps in my stomach.

Maybe these questions are necessary
to shake up the guilt
of what we have like a pillow
full of feathers sticky with death.

Question: are the homeseeking
also welcome here where three
families could live comfortably?

Move up a bit.

Maybe you'll eat some of the boar our neighbour
shot specially for your visit?
The meat has been in a marinade overnight.
There is also lamb that's more tender

I see myself freeze in the butcher's window
between the naked meat the blood
of which collects in puddles on metal dishes
with decorative edges of baroque tableware
from an age that still tries to determine something
but which is no longer understood.

I shut my eyes when my mother finally says no
to something else and the butcher asks
does she like sausage looking at me
and I think he means my mother who smiles at me encouragingly
and I say yes and force a thank-you through death
that rests like a pink slice in my mouth
a big unutterable I

I don't want to think about my mother's
egg cells which I must have too
and whether they lie heaped up like skulls
in catacombs or if they jump and whirl
and roll down the Fallopian tubes with a yell.

And when I no longer have any, daughter,
Where will the rumours go?

We are all red inside the hollow pelts
and somewhere there's a beating heart

On an online course I learned how to say sorry.
It starts with pr but sounds like zhayprasham.
The first time I said sorry to you
in your own language I had to weep Billie
before I knew it
that is what mothers do.

You're there anyway aren't you
if I say przepraszam.

Przepraszam that we didn't visit you more often
in the madhouse that later became a hospital
and you were a customer now though nothing had changed.

Przepraszam that I didn't call you any other name
that I didn't smuggle you out Billie.

We would have got used to your gloomy stories
your chockful plates
and your accusations we'd poisoned
pulled a fast one murdered you.

Maybe you'd have seen fewer ghosts then.
Fewer faces in the curtains
and you wouldn't have accused me
of being a spy for unnameable higher powers.

Przepraszam that I am a spy Billie

Find a tune for the still warm heart
of Chopin which his sister smuggled
under her crinoline from Paris to Warsaw
a bell in a swaying cupola.

Someone got there before me. He
travelled behind the heart and Ludwika.
Unemphatic and unforgettable
in an exhausting bodily prayer
he connects the heart with the body.

I can't go that far.

Don't make a competition of it.

My body remembers
nocturnes and mazurkas
that I dash off on my thighs.

There are two forms of mazurka slow and fast
and it is danced by at least four couples.

1    the heart and the body calm
2    unrest and driven up the river
3    struggle and the motherland quick quick
4    I and { }

Poland? The field I've never been to.
But how do you approach a country

excuses

and what's more: I no longer have a piano
because I distrust where that ballast
came from and why I ever started playing.
It is an instrument you can never
spontaneously bring to a party
it is anchored in your house.

Are you really grumbling about a piano?

Even the school my children go to
didn't want my piano for free!

They've already got five. No one plays them

It's a slow death
not going anywhere any more.

Stop showing off and play!

Scream.

Too much depends on the piano:
climbing up a ladder
that someone else placed.
What am I slamming shut if I close the lid?

Take care of your future!

How much does an electric piano cost?
With that money I could go to Poland

there

where is my heart?

and back.

Go!

Chop up a piano in blocks the size of dice.
Find two trolley cases the piano dice fit in.
Take them with you to Katowice
and shake them in a public square

Strew them like ashes.

Dice.

Na zdrowie

Wake all the miners and hug them
like family. Blow clouds of grit
out of their trumpets and trombones and march
behind the battered wind section. Let it sound
like bones or a raging torrent with rocks.

Create mayhem.

Like the mothers of the mothers
who disagree whether
you can come home and what the difference is between
in death and after.

Whether you can come home

Don't assume dice are unimportant
just because someone got there before you

seems fearless when he jumps into a ditch
with his back on fire or lets himself
be hoisted by a crane over his birthplace

angelic if it wasn't so deathly

in the Vistula sometimes vast as a sea
he is a heart

ser ce
serce
rce

in a jampot filled with cognac

splashing over the rim

and he plays the piano shamelessly

and he plays shamelessly

and he plays and he

unites slow and swift rivers in this heart

that flows at varying speeds

down the river

The wolves are growling under the table.
The loved ones and the dead stare at you
and still stare when you turn them over
like playing cards you expect something of.
You take a needle and blind us one by one.

The neighbour is a KGB agent
who taps your phone.
Who did you call? Own up! You've stolen
my scent from Cologne in that splendid bottle.
Did you know it was supplier to royalty
and that I smell like a queen? I know
you're hiding a camera in your earring.
You never wear such huge earrings.
Are you still not married to that German?
They never stay with you long.

Do all the old women who pass by
on slow boats down the Rhine to look at castles
eat dumplings tighten their perms
smell like princesses? Oh Lorelei
you should know. When the wolves are hard
on your heels and you defend yourself
with a breadknife they lock you up
with the others who are chased
you hiss and nod at a man who can't stop
nodding and sighing noisily strapped
to his chair and at the next visit you sit
nodding and sighing a perfect rhyme
that seems to be making fun of us but I
cannot shake shake us out

You break up
into voices I recognize one by one.

All you read now is stuff about royalty
the golden coach. Willem Alexander and Maxima
are getting babies you say like mosquitoes drawn to light.
Switch the light out!
Shouldn't you get a move on? At your age
I already had grandchildren. Sometimes you stroke
Maxima's rosy cheeks in a glossy mag. Sometimes you call her
a whore. Her father the devil her daughters changelings
but adorable all the same.

You leave their eyes unharmed

# Recent and uncollected poems

# Breaking Up Breaking

    I

*Is this the yoga?* a lean woman asks me
who's suddenly in my living room a mat
under her arm. She's taken off her shoes.

*The yoga* I say surprised. *No. That's further on.*
I close the door and lock it.

I hear someone booming though the letterbox
*there's no yoga here is there.*

NO YOGA I write with a red marker on three sheets
of paper that I stick on the window by the door.
I scribble a skull on it and an exclamation mark.

When a group of women shows up at the door
to ask if *noyoga* is a new course
I suspect that this isn't a coincidence.

*Yes of course come in* I can improvise a lesson.
A new life *welcome welcome.*

II

*You say the shutter speed required is too long.*
*The light that water sketches on the negatives*
*will be wiped out by the waves that follow.*

*In other words: it is impossible*
*to photograph the sea at night.*

You developed an increasingly deep black
that seemed to flail around.

Perhaps I wanted more.
Was this really water?
It is hard to see an end in the darkness

to waves I have witnessed.
Isn't at least the time visible
that we spent breaking up breaking?

I cover my eyes with my hands: I'm not here.
Do you see? In other words: do you see?

# Ha-Ha

It may be that I take myself too seriously
it may be that I myself
right here it may be. I don't exclude
that when it comes down to doing something
I take flight in words. It's no coincidence
that I keep on looking for a synonym for action.

I can blame my evasiveness
on education culture the book
a mask the lyric I: I? No
I can't go outside I'd rather read
about gardening than do something
in the garden while I have a garden and hands

and feet to dig holes and ditches
to sow trouble to lure insects
but I summon up all my courage in a folding chair
and read about a ha-ha. Enjoy
seeing coulisses sparkling
in the square of grass tucked between hedges

and fences of the silent garden where it is always festive
and the neighbour who peers through the shrubs
that he grew to keep out children and other riff-raff
to see if I've grown some nonindigenous plant
or let it blow in. As calm as I can I leaf through
*The History of Gardens*. The grass

beneath my feet starts smouldering.
Visitors to silent gardens are swarming in me
and it blazes with guardians of what or who
because I don't know how I can heave myself
over the hedge what am I supposed to do
with a faint mirror in a garden in a garden.

And I—exhumed to make the vista

from the stately home appealing
for someone lingering by the window
—am lying here with bated breath to give
an impression of boundless distance.
And I go on lying here. Roll in a sigh
in the earth that turns up turbulent life.

My sigh?

Look the worms provide the soil
with oxygen already. But who sees life

in a pit shaped like me.

# Night Ink

A tram rides through the treetops.

A woman is waving from the bridge
at a child sitting on the back of a bike.
He stretches his arms out wide
like oars and glides out of sight.
The circles in the water are searching
for a shore. The woman keeps on waving.

They are chestnuts says Adrian
he's set down his can of beer in a puddle
so he can hold up a grey ID card
that's hung by a ribbon round his neck.
His photo is on it. Look that's me.
Hair blowing in watery light.

Locust trees Bill is thinking or no
those are in the Wilhelminastraat.
He's sitting on a block with his feet
close together in the water. The same trees
are growing there on both sides
of the street. Here there's all kinds
mixed up together. You should talk
to Warren. Do you know him?

They aren't chestnuts says Adrian.

A woman is shuffling under the bridge
with her arms bent at an acute angle
to plough herself forward. She gazes
ahead as if she's on a journey
beyond the park. We follow
the path that she draws round the earth.

See how she runs in a calm
that rests in itself.

Dutch elms Tommy suggests. Rhombus
that's what they call me because I used
the Latin word for parallelogram
at school. I was sent out of the class
by my teacher who didn't know the word.
School was never really for me.

Without the trees I wouldn't be here.
Nor would you. Everything's linked to everything
like this grass with the roots
of these bathing trees patterns
in numerical series and water music.

Adrian says goodbye blowing a kiss.

I really must go.

Fiona gets off her bike
to take a look from nearby
at a tree floating away. White-knuckled hands
round the handlebars. Is that an olive?
I've never seen an olive tree.
Where are the olives?

Bill is wearing a pink sun hat
with a flower pattern.
I found this he grins.
I love the four-letter word
that begins with F.
FUCK!
No way. Yes, that too. FREE!
We nod.
The beer cans nod along.

Adrian returns to shake hands.

In Kenya says Johnny the tree is the place
where the family comes together.
I don't know where my family is.
It's nature I miss most of all.
I sleep on the street but the trees
remain. Look, there's water
running there. You can wash and drink
from the source. A heron stands stock-still
amid the tin cans in the stream.

I never see rollerbladers coming
they show up out of nowhere and roll
right through you. Do they know each other
or are they all on their own?

Adrian is sitting on the far side.
He is showing his card to someone else.

Gloria sings a song in a deep voice
and brushes her dog in time
with the melody. She cleans the brush
and keeps the soft hairs in a bag.
Branches and park weed get entangled
and the animal that tugs on its lead.
We dive from the bridge. Plunge
beneath trees that bear our names
written in night ink
in this park that surely sinks.

# Song of the Garbage Man

On the back of the truck
no one can get me down.
I'm coming for the loaded
pockets of the town.

Should one of them burst
I see a life a body replete
in shards and peelings
spilling out on the street.

Anyone got a problem
if I drive the garbage truck
to the fruit machines
just to try my luck.

Bunches in a row
and luring lemons roll
as they pass by in pairs.
Coins jingle jingle

less when I have to go
home with empty pockets
till the next truck full
of chances waits.

On the back of the truck
no one can get me down.
I'm coming for the loaded
pockets of the town.

# The Borders of Europe

*Europa* (1931–32) was the first film by Stefan Themerson (1910–88) and Franciszka Themerson (1907–88). It is based on the antifascist poem *Europa* (1925) by Anatol Stern that he had dedicated to 'the tragedy, the squalor, the wisdom and the decadence of Europe'. Thought to have been lost during the Second World War, the film was reconstructed in 1983. In 2019 the original was rediscovered, allowing for the original and the reconstruction to be compared.


A standing nude was constructed
the lower part replaced by a loaf of bread
slit open under a new angle.

A sculpture of a head was devised.
Two female faces on long legs
a motionless heart and a black surface
of not knowing—what do you think Malevich?—
survived a long time. Can the thundering speed
of images offer anything against the boots
I thought I saw myself

—reconstructed or invented Europe—
they trample the blazing grass
that was already flattened the boots they stomp
splashes out of the slowly dissolving mist.

A boxer triumphs without sound
the victorious fist held high
a heart beats shrinks beats
a dancing jellyfish pipe
languishes clock child apple
over man eats apple.

Who does the flag with blood stains belong to?
Who doesn't the flag with blood stains belong to?

A high hollow sinks
because of Fascism that can be
reconstructed like a lost film.

And what will be invented this time?

The eyes of a man consist of pure light
and someone cuts the apple
someone eats the apple
someone

stands with clenched fists.

Another man eats fatty meat
is that him the Fascist that must be him
for breakfast with bulging neck folds
what's he shouting who's he shouting after?

Clouds megaphones shake in the rhythm
of eternal stamping
so as to graze stamp-shock
in just enough frames a minute
to show us that this life
is a clash of order disorder
order in the ugly mug of the man
who gobbles down gulped up wads
news items assail the crowds—
Scream back! it screams in the poet.
Stand up everyone but the poet with clenched fists
can't find the right tone
he doesn't know what his images are.

A heart pulsates like a broken light bulb
cannons soldiers barbed wire spider

body on cross yes-man
whose are these stripes what flag
bears the keys of a lost piano—

so that men like him
and the men he wants to be
who may be the same men
in the eyes of the self-assured
who want to make a better world
by taking themselves as the norm

are consumed by the moment
that the light in her eyes
seems like love or is and the light
that caught her meet

Apples are cut on the conveyor belt.
A broad public cut from the repetition
of one person eats the apple slices.
Is that us? Where has the hand gone to
that found the core of the apple and what
do the typewriter keys destroy.

There is a moment of calm and then another
in clear outlines of a ruler a hand
a building buildings skyscrapers
or century centuries lifetime old age
the heart s o s in reverse
but a spreading branch squeezes
and bare feet run through the grass.

The swaying branches the leaves
are distorted by speed
so that pieces of apples a seismograph
and a blade of grass

between the paving stones pushes
the cobbles aside
to let a tree grow.

The trees fall over.
The cities fall.
Mouths forced open scream
fall in a falling silence
fleeing feet
legs dynamite beautiful eyes gaze love
city falls the body hesitates.

Is it enough that we are
stammering witnesses of this Europe
what do you still mean
if image after image I am
persuaded that watching
eating an apple
that looks like a host
like the body
of someone with good intentions
makes complicit with war
even if you turn off the tv.

And the fleeing who die unnumbered
forced back shot back
allowed because seen
does this cross your borders Europe
and nobody to reconstruct them.

That I doubt if I must be we
and what remains of us
if we can't remember
what images we needed
to fight against what silenced us
if we don't know what images

we must choose now.

And the reconstruction will take its time
the reconstruction operates
in a vacuum the reconstruction
constructs while we are looking
for the right word.

Eyes look upward
a sky full of panic
falls hurtling in a gut

a show diver takes flight.

# Acknowledgements

A number of these translations have been published online on the Rotterdam Poetry International website. Some translations have been published previously in *Poetry Wales*, *The Enchanting Verses*, issue 26, *PN Review* nos. 242 and 261, *Staying Human*, (Bloodaxe Books, 2020), 'Lonely Funerals' (Arc Publications, 2018), the Dutch issue of the online journals, The High Window (https://thehighwindowpress.com/2017/06/03/dutch-poetry/) and the *Loch Raven Review* (https://thelochravenreview.net/loch-raven-review-volume-13-no-2-2017/) and in an anthology of Dutch poetry, *Rinkeldekinkel* (ed. Rob Schouten, Milkweed Editions, Minneapolis, 2021).

'In memory of Chengian Chen', 'Looking for you' and 'Song of the Garbage Man' were written for the Lonely Funeral project that commissions poems to be written and read out at the funerals of those without friends and relatives.

www.ingramcontent.com/pod-product-compliance
Lightning Source LLC
Chambersburg PA
CBHW031420160426
43196CB00008B/1001